S0-CFN-348

This Book Belongs To:

Glenda Biord

29

30

32

33

34

38

39

40

41

42

45

46

48

49

50

55

56

58

60

61

66

67

68

69

70

Dear Bride to be,

Every bride longs to create a beautiful, memorable wedding day. It is a once in a life time opportunity, she hopes, to express her love for her groom, family and friends. She desires to look her best, have all the essential details of the ceremony and reception covered, and walk down the aisle with a feeling of inner confidence and calm.

The first section of this book includes all the basic information you need to do the wedding of your dreams plus many creative and cost saving hints. The second part of the book includes many spectacular, cost saving projects you can make to add to the splendor and charm of your wedding. With a little creativity and some help from family and friends, you can create a glorious wedding and have money left over for other things.

The days of preparation are opportunities to use your imagination and be creative. Wearing a headpiece that you have patiently made with your own hands, or holding a bouquet of flowers you carefully and artfully arranged will add to your feeling of calmness and confidence.

Engagement Announcements for the Newspaper

Contact the society editors of all the papers in which you desire to announce your engagement, and specify the date on which you want it to be printed. If you need your photo returned, provide your name, address, and "please return" on the back of the picture, as well as a self-addressed, stamped envelope. The newspapers probably won't send you copies of your announcements, so remember to look for them around the day you have requested them to appear.

SAMPLE ENGAGEMENT ANNOUNCEMENT

Please print on _____

Mr. and Mrs._____
(your parents names)

of _____
(their city, if out of town)

Announce the engagement of their daughter,

_____
(your first and middle names)

to_____
(your fiances first and last names)

the son of Mr. and Mrs. _____

_____
(your fiances parents' names)

of_____
(fiances parents' city)

❏ At the present time, the wedding date has not been decided upon. (or)

❏ The wedding will take place in _____
(month of wedding).

Make copies, fill in, and mail to newspapers.

Wedding Announcements for the Newspaper

It is customary to publish the details of a formal wedding in your hometown newspapers. If you and your groom have studio photographs taken in your wedding attire before the wedding, have the photographer take some in black and white for your newspaper announcement. You can prepare your announcement before the wedding, and ask your maid of honor to send out the information while you are away on your honeymoon. Make sure she gets copies for you.

"Come to the edge," he said.

They said, "We are afraid."

"Come to the edge," he said.

They came.

He pushed them,

and they flew.

– GUILLAUME APOLLINAIRE

Setting the Wedding Time and Date

June is still the most popular wedding month, then August, July, May, September, October, April and December. Spring is a highly favored season to marry, so locations and services might need to be booked well in advance. If your first choice is for an outdoor wedding, the possibility of rain needs to be factored into your plans. Give yourself a full year to prepare for a large, formal wedding and at least three months for a smaller, informal one.

Printing Needs

Wedding Invitations

Order the wedding invitations about three months in advance. This allows time for delivery, addressing and mailing. They should go out from four to six weeks before the wedding. Formal invitations are not necessary for a small, informal wedding. A brief note can take the place of a printed invitation when fewer than fifty guests are invited. Order more than you think you will need.

Wedding Announcements

Wedding announcements are sent to acquaintances, business associates and people you know who are not able to attend. An announcement does not obligate them to give you a gift. It simply lets them know of your marriage. Mail them soon after the wedding.

Ceremony Programs

The ceremony program is a detail that can communicate a lot of love. It is a place where you can share how you met and quotes on marriage that express your ideas and feelings. It is an opportunity to be with your guests in a very intimate, personal way. It shows the order in which things take place: songs, prayers, scriptures to be read and the names of the ushers and attendants.

Thank you Cards and Personal Stationery

One of the benefits of printing your own stationery is you can choose the size. Have your stationery printed on a half sheet, and use it for both personal letters and thank you notes. Also, if you are sending out a number of thank you notes, writing them on paper that has your letterhead makes it a lot easier for you, and is a convenient way to remind people of your new name and address.

Legal Details

Call your city offices to determine where to apply for your marriage license. It may be at city hall, a town clerk's office or a marriage license bureau. Each state has its own requirements regarding the age of consent, blood tests, necessary documents and the length of time the license is valid. Ask when you should apply, and how long your license will be valid after it is issued.

If you are changing your name, change it on your driver's license, car registration, voter's registration, social security card, passport, stocks, bonds, property titles, leases, employee records, medical insurance, taxes and at your post office.

Are your belongings adequately insured? Does it cover your wedding gifts and rings? What about medical and life insurance? Do either of you need a pre-nuptial agreement? Plan the future custody of children either of you may be bringing into the marriage. Do you need to make out wills, change beneficiaries and change the names on your bank accounts and bank cards?

"Love does not consist in gazing into each other's eyes, but in looking together in the same direction."
— Exupery

Choosing Your Ceremony and Reception Locations

When selecting your ceremony site, keep in mind the distance to your reception location. Will transportation of your wedding party to the reception be difficult? Is the parking adequate? Make an appointment with your officiant to discuss the policies of the church, temple or synagogue of your choice.

Questions to Ask

- Do you have to belong to the church to be married in the church?

- How much are the fees, and how long can the ceremony last?

- Do they have facilities for the reception. Is there an additional charge?

- How many people will the church accommodate?

- Are there any restrictions concerning decorations?

- May rice, birdseed or flower petals be tossed?

- Can you change the wording of the marriage ceremony?

- Can you include vows, prayers or songs of your own choice?

- Are there any rules regarding photography and videography in the chapel?

- Are there any music restrictions?

- Do they have dressing rooms for the bride and groom?

Some Ideas

- Buy pre-packaged cards, or use stationery and hand write each guest's invitation. It is a very personal way to invite friends and family.

- Include the reception and R.S.V.P. information on the ceremony invitation. Use invitations that require only one stamp.

- Decorate with potted plants or cut flowers that are in season. Use one flower and some greenery in a bud vase as centerpieces for the tables.

- Buy silk flowers for centerpieces, and arrange them yourself. They can be prepared well in advance of the wedding, and can be used later in your new home. Or, give them away as gifts to your attendants.

- Rent your own helium equipment, and have someone in the bridal party fill balloons. Purchase colorful, Mylar bags from a party store, fill them with sand, and tie clusters of balloons to the tops. Use them to decorate the reception.

- Have the ceremony and the reception in the same place. It will cut the cost and inconvenience of transporting the wedding party, and will be easier for guests to come to the reception. The decorations for the ceremony can easily be transported for use at the reception.

- Have the reception at your family's or a friend's home.

- Borrow cutlery, punch bowls, coffee pots and serving dishes instead of renting them.

- Use paper tablecloths and napkins, plates, cups and utensils instead of renting silver, linens and china.

- Have a morning or afternoon reception and serve punch and cake or cocktails and hors d'oeuvres instead of lunch or dinner.

- Ask family members if they want to prepare and serve the food instead of having it catered. Have friends help with setting up, serving and bartending.

- Invite only close friends and family.

- Have a professional photographer take pictures of the ceremony, and ask friends to take pictures and videos during the reception.

- Have a musician friend play something beautiful before the ceremony, and have a friend sing 'your' song.

- Purchase tapes of the music you want played during the reception, and ask a friend to be the disc jockey.

The Bridal Party

The wedding attendants give both the bride and groom moral support as well as practical assistance with the numerous details of the wedding.

The maid or matron of honor helps the bride with details. She helps with the invitations, goes shopping with her, helps decorate, facilitates the bridesmaids' fittings and helps organize them on the wedding day. She keeps the groom's ring until the appropriate time during the ceremony, and signs the wedding certificate as a legal witness. She helps the bride dress, and assists her with her train and veil at the altar. She helps the bride prepare for her exit at the reception.

The Bridesmaids provide a beautiful background for your wedding. They attend all pre-wedding parties and assist with some of the pre-wedding errands. They may have a bridal shower for the bride on their own or with members of the family.

The Ushers arrive at the ceremony site an hour or so early to greet and seat early guests. After the ceremony, they escort the bridesmaids out of the church. It is not necessary to have the same number of ushers as bridesmaids.

The bride's mother may assist with any aspect of the wedding. She compiles a wedding invitation list, and helps address the envelopes. She is the official hostess at the reception.

The bride's father rides with the bride to the ceremony, and escorts her down the aisle. He stands in the receiving line at the reception.

The groom's parents usually host the rehearsal dinner. It can be in their home, or in a favorite restaurant or club. They welcome the bride and her family into the family with a note, a phone call or an invitation to lunch or dinner if they haven't met before. They can be as involved in the wedding as you would like them to be.

The ringbearer is usually an adorable little boy who follows the bride down the aisle holding a lacy pillow with golden wedding rings tied to it.

The flower girl brings up the end of the line of wedding participants. She carries a small decorated basket filled with flower petals, which she scatters as she walks down the aisle. If you have two flower girls they can carry a garland.

Honorary participants are in charge of details that allow the wedding to run smoothly. They can act as host or hostess at the reception site until the family members arrive. Sometimes the photographs of the bridal party can take forty-five minutes or so. They give last minute directions to the reception site, help decorate the reception room, ask guests to sign the guest book and take care of the gifts.

Wedding Attire

The Bridal Gown

Finding a gown that suits your personality, flatters your figure and is within your budget may take time. Then again, the first one you try on may turn out to be the perfect dress. Make an appointment to make sure you have the time and help you need to select your gown. Wear a strapless bra so you can try on a variety of dresses. Wear shoes the same heel height you will be wearing on your wedding day. If you plan to wear a special necklace, earrings, heirloom jewelry or gloves, bring them with you.

Let your gown assistant know how much you plan to spend. If you fall in love with a gown that is beyond your budget, explore possibilities with the salon owner. See if you can find a similar dress that costs less or a simpler one that you or a dressmaker can decorate on your own for less than it would cost to buy ready made. Maybe you can find a similar style in a less expensive fabric. Ask for a price quote on alterations, and inquire about special payments or layaway plans.

Bring a friend and a camera with you when you shop for your dress. She can take pictures of you in the styles you are considering. When you see how you photograph in the different gowns it may influence your decision.

Specify in writing the store policy for gown storage and pickup. Make sure the dress manufacturer and style number, size and color is on the bill of sale. List the embellishments, sequins, pearls and lace to be added. Specify special order alterations and the delivery date. Some bridal salons include one fitting in the cost of the gown. Be sure to ask about additional charges for any special alterations, including headpieces and veils.

Styles of Wedding Gowns

SCOOP COLLAR

SWEETHEART COLLAR

LEG OF MUTTON
SLEEVE

FULL OVERSIZE SKIRT

CATHEDRAL TRAIN

PORTRAIT COLLAR

NATURAL BODICE

JULIETTE SLEEVE

SHEATH

CHAPEL TRAIN

OFF THE SHOULDER
COLLAR

DROPPED BODICE

STRAIGHT SLEEVE

FULL TAILORED

FLOOR TRAIN

WEDDING BAND
COLLAR

BASQUE BODICE

LONGPOINT SLEEVE

MERMAID

SWEEP TRAIN

The Bride's Headpiece

If you plan to wear your hair up for your wedding, wear it up when you shop. Have your friend take photos of you in the different styles you like. If you are planning to wear it during the reception, choose one that will be comfortable in a social situation or one with a removable veil. Or, you can change to a smaller headpiece, like a comb decorated with flowers and pearls or a large bow decorated with fresh, fabric or silk flowers. Practice hairstyles that look best with both the veil and a smaller decorative accent, if you choose to change for the reception.

Most craft stores have a bridal department with a consultant or a designer that will assist you in selecting everything you need to create a beautiful headpiece.

Wedding Accessories

Wear sheer beige, champagne, white or ivory stockings. They should match your shoes and wedding gown. There are also beautiful wedding hose with appliques and lace designs. It is an important accessory, especially when you remove your garter during the reception.

Wear comfortable shoes. Make sure the heels are not too high. A pump style shoe in silk or satin, dyed to match your dress is a classic, wedding shoe. You can also decorate your shoes with matching lace, pearls and sequins.

Wear them around the house to break them in before the wedding. Decorated ballet slippers can be purchased at some bridal salons. Or, you can buy plain ballet slippers at a dance store, and decorate them to match your gown.

Wedding Keepsakes

Ringbearer pillows come in a variety of styles, colors and shapes. They can be purchased at bridal salons, specialty pillow shops or through mail order. You may want to make your own. (See page 68.)

Personalized toasting glasses with ribbons and flowers make great keepsakes. Keep them in a special place, and bring them out to be used for toasting on anniversaries down the years of your married life. (See page 44.)

A decorated cake knife adds a special feeling to an already special day. Tie ribbons around the handle of a family heirloom, borrow a beautiful cake cutting knife from a friend or relative, or purchase one of your own. (See page 44.)

The guest book will be a nostalgic reminder, full of the names and feelings of all the friends and relatives that helped you celebrate your wedding day. Make it beautiful by adding touches of lace, ribbons and pearls. Some shops specialize guest books by embroidering your names on the front in the colors of your wedding. Put Name, Address, Zip and Phone Number at the tops of the pages if your guest book lacks these instructions. (See page 32.)

Preserving Your Wedding Gown

Before the wedding, take your gown to the cleaners and inquire about their preserving procedure. If you prefer to preserve it yourself, don't leave it hanging on a hanger or wrapped in plastic. Remove protective shields and bra inserts, and fold the dress with layers of acid free tissue in-between the folds. Then, wrap it in a white muslin sheet and store in a cedar chest or a lined drawer. Air it out from time to time, and refold it in different places making sure to add layers of tissue each time. Do not add moth balls. The fumes can damage the fibres of the gown.

Some Ideas

- Special wedding products can be found in craft stores. Clear sequins that give off a bright sparkle, but not the color of iridescent sequins, are now available. These sequins, often found on ready-made wedding gowns, can be used to coordinate your headpiece and other accessories with your gown.

- Make your own headpiece.

- Buy a ready-to-wear dress or a street length dress that doesn't require alterations.

- Look through dresses that are on sale or purchase samples or discontinued styles.

- Have the dress you like made in a less expensive fabric. Some of the polyesters come in beautiful shades and have silky or taffeta textures.

- Purchase your gown from someone whose wedding was cancelled. Look in the newspaper or inquire at bridal shops.

- Sew your own gown, or purchase a simple, inexpensive gown from a salon, bead your own lace appliques, and add them to the gown.

- Wear your mother's, sister's or a friend's gown. It adds great sentiment to the wedding.

- Borrow your accessories from a close friend or relative.

- Rent a gown. Many stores rent both dressy, formal wear and wedding gowns. Check your yellow pages.

- Ask about package discounts. Many stores offer discounts if you purchase the bridesmaid's dresses from them.

- Make your own accessories: garter, cake top, ring pillow, toasting glasses, guest book etc.

- Carry a single perfect flower with ribbons streaming, and have your attendants do the same.

Wedding Flowers

There are many variations on what the bride carries down the aisle. She can hold the family bible decorated with flowing, white satin ribbons and flowers, a decorated parasol, a Victorian nosegay surrounded with antique lace or a tussie mussie (hand tied bouquet in which the stems are tied together, then cut to a uniform, convenient-to-carry length). Your florist can wire or glue together individual petals of a flower in a cluster to create a full, magnificent blossom on a single stem. Or, you can carry a single, perfect flower with ribbons tied to the stem.

If you plan to carry a bouquet, ask your florist about making one for you to keep and one to throw. After the reception ask your maid of honor to place your bouquet in a box and completely cover it with borax or silica gel. Add your groom's boutonniere. This process absorbs the moisture while protecting the color and the petals of the flowers. By the time you return from the honeymoon, (at least a week) your bridal flowers will be preserved.

Or, you can have her separate the flowers into individual stems and dry them in silica gel or borax. Later on you can use them to make a wreath to hang in your new home as a reminder of your wedding day. If you plan to have pre-wedding photographs taken, discuss the details of having your bridal bouquet before the wedding. If the photo session is a day or so before, you may be able to use the same bouquet.

Consider wearing flowers in your hair rather than a headpiece. They may be worn alone or as a delicate wreath with a veil attached to the back. A second-time-bride may prefer to wear orchids or gardenias in her hair. The bride may wear a headpiece to the ceremony, remove it for the reception and wear a flower decorated comb for dancing and mingling with her guests.

The bridesmaids' bouquets are smaller versions of the bridal bouquet with added touches of flowers or ribbons in colors that match their dresses. The maid of honor's bouquet should set her apart from the bridesmaids by being larger or in a different color.

A delicate head wreath made of real or silk flowers with ribbons streaming down the back looks beautiful on the flower girl. She can carry a nosegay or a small decorated basket full of rose petals to be scattered in the path behind the wedding procession.

Both the mothers and grandmothers are honored guests and should be presented with corsages before the ceremony. They can be pinned on their dresses, worn on their wrist or attached to their handbags. Ask them what color and kind of flowers they prefer and what style corsage would be best for them. All the men in the bridal party wear boutonniere. The groom's boutonniere is a little different from the rest to set him apart.

Have a written contract that includes when and where the flowers will be delivered and the total cost. Most florists require a deposit. Pay in full when you have received all the flowers.

Flowers for the Ceremony

In elaborate formal weddings, large bouquets are placed on either side of the altar, and ribbons and flowers line the aisle. There are many just as beautiful and less costly options.

Some Ideas

- Rent live ficus trees and potted palms to surround the area where the ceremony will take place, or purchase 'silk' green or flowering trees.

- Add tiny stationary lights to the branches of the trees to enhance the feeling of celebration. Add potted flowers (silk or live) amidst the greenery. Put some on boxes for a high low effect. Add fresh flowers from a nursery. Leave them in the plastic containers, put netting around them, and put plastic underneath to protect the floor.

- You can also adorn the window sills with hanging gardens made of silk or fresh flowers and leaves. Attach sprays of flowers to the aisle posts on the rows reserved for special guests or relatives. Drape garlands of white netting with white satin ribbons and touches of small flowers or baby's breath and ferns.

- Rent an arch made of twigs, metal or wood. Decorate it with fresh or silk flowers and lots of netting and ribbons. Rent tall candelabras to stand on either side or large urns filled with elaborate garden arrangements set on pedestals, pillars or stands. Look in the yellow pages for bridal rentals or ask friends and relatives where to find what you need. Your florist is a good source of information.

- Talk to your clergyman to see if there are any restrictions regarding placement of flowers and decorations in the facility. If your wedding takes place on the same day as another bride's wedding, you may be able to share the cost of the altar flowers with her.

- If you plan to use the flowers at the ceremony to add to the decorations at the reception site, ask someone to be responsible for transporting them after the photography and videography are finished.

Reception Flowers

Flowers on the head table, centerpieces on the individual tables, an arrangement for the buffet, a small arrangement next to the guest book, one in the powder room, flowers on the cake table, trees in back of the receiving line and lots of candles and balloons will transform a reception hall into a palace ballroom. Coordinate the colors of the table linens and flowers with the colors in the bridal party.

Some Ideas

- Place votive candles in plastic bowls filled with sand, and line the walkways to the reception.

- Use tiny lights wrapped in netting and drape them over doorways.

- Have childhood pictures of the bride and groom framed and sitting next to the guest book.

- Spend an afternoon with a photographer taking pictures of you and your groom posing on the beach, playing golf...whatever you enjoy doing together. Make a collage of the photos with captions on a large piece of poster board, and place it on an easel near the cake table.

- Search out wholesale flower companies and make the arrangements yourself. Ask a friend with some flower arranging experience to help you.

- Use lots of helium filled balloons with trailing ribbons and flowers to decorate the bar, cake table, guest table etc. They are inexpensive and add a feeling of celebration, especially in a large reception hall.

- Use lots of greenery. Garlands and trees, both silk and fresh, can provide a beautiful background for both the ceremony and the reception.

The Wedding Cake

Wedding cakes come in all sizes and flavors. Find out if the price of the cake includes transporting it to the reception. Some brides order groom's cakes, a small, standard size cake in his favorite flavor. It is placed next to the wedding cake, and small portions are served at the same time or given to the guests in small boxes to take home as favors.

The following extraordinary chocolate pecan cake can be made the day before and stored in the refrigerator overnight. Use a 13" X 9" size pan for the smaller size. Make the larger cake in one 18" X 26" size pan and a 13" X 9" size sheet cake pan, or use three 13" X 9" sizes.

If you use the three similar sizes, place them side by side, and decorate with small bouquets in between and around the cakes. Or, have the center cake slightly raised. Any bakery shop has plastic circles in various sizes that you can purchase to put on top of the center cake to add decorations. Some fresh flowers, a beautiful white bow, doves, a bride and groom... use anything you like to decorate your cake.

Chocolate Pecan Wedding Cake

For 15 people	For 50 people
2 Cups sugar	14 Cups sugar
2 Cups flour	14 Cups flour
½ Cup butter	3 ½ Cups butter
6 Tblsp. cocoa	42 Tblsp. cocoa
½ Cup oil	3 ½ Cup oil
1 Cup water	7 Cups water
½ Cup buttermilk	3 ½ Cups buttermilk
1 Tsp. baking soda	7 Tsp. baking soda
½ Tsp. salt	3 ½ Tsp. salt
2 Eggs	14 Eggs (7 Tblsp. egg replacer)
1 ½ Tsp. vanilla	10 ½ Tsp. vanilla
	(3 tblsp. & 1 1/2 tsp.)

Grease a 9" X 13" cake pan for the smaller cake. Grease three 9" X 13" cake pans for the larger cake. Set oven at 350 degrees.

Sift sugar, flour, salt and baking soda into a large bowl. Mix well. Melt butter in a saucepan and add cocoa, oil and water. Stir constantly, and bring to a rapid boil. (If you are using an egg substitute, use some of the water to liquefy the egg replacer, and use the remaining water in the saucepan.) Pour over the dry ingredients, and stir well.

Beat in the buttermilk, eggs (or liquefied egg replacer) and vanilla. Pour into greased pans, and bake each for 30 minutes, or until done. Allow cake to cool before adding frosting.

Chocolate Butter Frosting

For 15 people	For 50 people
1 Stick butter	6 Sticks butter
3 Tblsp. cocoa	18 Tblsp. cocoa
4 Tblsp. buttermilk	1 ¼ Cups buttermilk
3 Cups powdered sugar	15 Cups powdered sugar
1 Tsp. vanilla	2 Tblsp. vanilla
Optional	
1 Cup chopped pecans	6 Cups chopped pecans

Melt butter and add cocoa in heavy saucepan, stirring constantly. Remove from heat, and add buttermilk and sugar. Stir in vanilla and pecans. Spread over cake while frosting is still warm.

"To keep your marriage brimming
with love in the loving cup,
whenever you're wrong, admit it;
whenever you're right,
shut up."
– OGDEN NASH

Food for the Reception

If you decide to have your reception catered, contact a variety of caterers before you make your final decision. Sample their food, and get all the details in the form of a contract. If your reception is held at an Inn or a hotel, ask about their catering services.

Questions to Ask

• What is their cancellation policy ?

• Is there a delivery fee, and is the gratuity included in their price ?

• Will you need to hire a waiter, or do they supply dining service ?

• Will the waiters cut and serve the wedding cake and the champagne for toasting the bride and groom ?

• Are there any additional fees ?

If you choose to provide your own food, consider a buffet with lots of fresh vegetables and dips. Provide bowls of whipped cream, chocolate, powdered sugar and sour cream for fresh strawberries, bananas, apples and citrus fruits.

Purchase long wooden skewers, and make fruit shish kebabs out of melons, grapes and strawberries. Insert the skewers into a carved out, upside down watermelon. Surround the base with flowers.

Make platters filled with different cheeses and cold cuts, and have a variety of delicious breads in decorated baskets. Provide champagne, sparkling cider, coffee and tea for your beverages.

If you want to provide a more elaborate spread, make a delicious tomato soup that can be served hot or cold, depending upon the weather. Have a caterer provide roasted or barbecued meats for an even more elaborate buffet. Soup tureens, platters, dishes and cutlery, linens and chairs can be rented from a party supply business. Or, use paper and plastic.

The Best Basil Tomato Soup

For 40 People
1 ½ Cubes of butter
4 Yellow onions
6 Green peppers
½ Bunch celery
8 Dried bay leaves
1 ½ Tblsp. fresh grated ginger
1 Large bunch fresh basil
3-4 Tblsp. oregano
3 ½ Tblsp. salt
2 Tsp. pepper
¾ Cup sugar
6 Large, fresh tomatoes
5 Large potatoes
2 Large cans chopped tomatoes
7 Large zucchini
5 Qts. boiling water
Chopped cilantro or parsley for garnish

Optional: 1 Pint of sour cream for people to add, as desired, if soup is served cold.

Peel, cut in half, and thinly slice the onions. Finely chop the green pepper, celery and fresh tomatoes (or use a food processor). Peel the potatoes, cut into small pieces, cover with water, and cook until they fall apart. Open the cans of chopped tomatoes. Wash the fresh basil, and finely chop. Cut the zucchinis in half and thinly slice. Grate the ginger.

Saute the onions in the butter in a large, heavy soup pot until soft. Add the bay leaves, basil, oregano, ginger, fresh tomatoes, sugar and salt. Stir constantly. Put the water on to boil.

Add the canned tomatoes, potatoes and zucchinis. Add the boiling water, stir and allow to simmer for 1/2 hour. When done, add the pepper. Garnish with chopped parsley or cilantro before serving either hot or cold.

Setting Up the Bar

An easy way to provide refreshments for your guests is to have two kinds of punch, non-alcoholic and alcoholic. Place them on a decorated table with a supply of fresh glasses, and let guests help themselves Or, have drinks available for your guests to order on there own at a specific refreshment center.

Photography

Your photographer is one of the most important people at your wedding. Choose him or her carefully. Make appointments with many photographers before you decide upon one. Ask to see sample wedding albums or a set of proofs from a recent wedding. Look for variety in the poses and backgrounds. Is he or she able to capture subtle feelings and relaxed features? Are you happy with the lighting, sharpness and composition of the photographs? You need to feel comfortable working together, and you need to feel confident that your photographer can do the job. Start looking for a good photographer months before the wedding.

Clarify your expectations with a written contract that specifies the time of arrival, the number and kinds of pictures to be taken and the time of departure. Many photographers offer a wedding package, which includes a number of pictures in various sizes. Ask about the cost of duplicate albums for your parents, and how long they hold onto the negatives in case you want to purchase more pictures in the future.

Many bride and grooms have a posed wedding photograph taken in the photographer's studio a few days before the wedding. This is a good time to test your headpiece and makeup. Your bridal photograph will look as if it was taken on your wedding day if you bring all your accessories and your flowers. Have the florist make you a duplicate bouquet, or it may be possible to use the same flowers if care is taken to preserve their freshness. Have some black and white photos taken for newspaper announcements. Most papers ask for a 5" X 7" glossy print.

Wear natural looking makeup. Color film intensifies bold shades. Take your time, and apply it carefully. Stay out of the sun before any photo sessions. A sunburn, even when it is covered with makeup, is seen by the eye of the camera. Wear a foundation, blush on the tops of your cheek bones and a natural color for your lips. Outline your lips with a slightly darker shade of the same color.

Line your eyes at the base of your lashes with a delicate touch. You just want to emphasize the shape, not call undo attention. Shape your brows, and darken them a little, if needed. Apply eye shadow sparingly, and blend it in. Lightly dust your makeup with loose or pressed powder, and pat the excess from your face and neck with a damp cotton ball. Add mascara to your lashes.

If you are not used to wearing makeup and lack confidence in applying it for your photos, consider having your makeup done by a professional, not only for the pre-wedding photos, but for the wedding as well. Have your hairdresser arrange your hair around your headdress.

Choose someone from both the bride and groom's family to guide the photographer to take pictures of special people and groups of people. He/she will not have time to figure out which people are family and close friends, nor will he/she know which people to photograph together. Some houses of worship do not allow flashbulbs or photographs to be taken around the altar or during the ceremony. Let your photographer know the protocol.

Some Ideas

- Have Polaroid pictures taken of the guests with the bride and groom to be given as favors.

- Have throw away cameras placed on each of the tables for the guests to take pictures. Ask someone to collect all the cameras after the reception is over.

- Take your camera with you whenever you attend to the details of your wedding. Take before and after pictures of the church and the reception. Have someone take a picture of you and your groom buying your wedding rings, getting your marriage license, trying on wedding dresses, choosing bridesmaids's dresses, at the florist and mailing your invitations. Make a pre-wedding album, and have someone bring it to the reception. It can sit on a special table next to a flower arrangement. Make sure someone takes it home after the reception.

Videography

Videotaping is becoming standard procedure for capturing weddings for future viewing. Your photographer may know of someone. Look for ads in bridal magazines. Set up appointments to view samples of their work, so you can see if the color is clear and not too bright or muddy. Are the voices audible, the pans smooth and the editing professional? Work with your professional to structure a plan and a package that will commemorate your wedding and be within your budget.

The wedding day, from beginning to end, could be recorded in a documentary style showing the bride dressing and guests arriving. Two cameras could be used to record the vows and conversation at the altar as well as the couple walking down the aisle. Guests can be interviewed at the reception giving their secrets to a lasting marriage, or advice praising the single life. Stories about childhood or college days can be captured on tape.

The least expensive way to video tape your wedding is to have a family member or friend shoot the ceremony and recep-

tion with one camera. This eliminates the need for editing, and you can take the tape on your honeymoon.

Questions to Ask

- How many cameras and what type of editing will be included in the price. Will titles and music be included ?

- Will they use cordless, remote microphones during the ceremony. What kind of lights will they use, and will it intrude upon the wedding ?

- Will they do interviews with your guests ?

- How much are extra tapes ?

Wedding Transportation

A romantic getaway vehicle is the first choice for most couples. See if your budget allows you to rent a limousine to take you and your father to the church and you and your groom to the reception.

Look in the yellow pages for a reputable firm. Read their insurance policy to check its' validity and to see if it is up to date. Look at the cars, and make sure that the one you choose is the one that arrives on your wedding day. Meet the driver, and make sure he knows the area.

Most companies have a one to two hour minimum. To save money, have one limo pick you up and take you to the ceremony and reception, and another come and take you to your final destination. Ask about special wedding packages.

Wedding Gifts

Registering gift preferences is something the bride and groom should do together. Take your time deciding on your crystal, china and silver. Talk to your groom and discuss your preferences in decorating and entertaining. Register different things in different stores to avoid duplications, and register a variety of gifts in a wide price range. Your maid of honor and your families can let people know where you are registered.

Keep an up-to-date gift record. Write down the date of arrival, a description of the gift and how you felt about it. Note the name and address of the sender, and the date the thank you note was sent. Save the packages with mailing labels for awhile in case you need to exchange or return the gift. If a gift arrives damaged, notify the store rather than the sender.

Prepare a table at the reception for gifts, and arrange to have someone there with a roll of scotch tape to secure the cards to the gifts. Another way to keep track of gifts is by having each gift bearing guest sign a numbered sheet. The same number can be written on the gift.

"A wise lover values not so much the gift of the lover as the love of the giver."
– THOMAS KEMPIS

The Rehearsal

Anywhere from a few days before to the eve of the wedding, you, your groom, clergyman, close members of the family and all the members of the wedding, including ushers, readers, singers and musicians will gather at the ceremony site to go through the procedure of the wedding. After the rehearsal, the groom's parents traditionally host a rehearsal dinner. The entire wedding party, immediate families and clergy are invited. Some couples plan the rehearsal a couple of days before the wedding, so they can enjoy the party without worrying about having to get a good nights sleep.

Allow the officiant or church coordinator to take charge. He or she knows exactly where each person should be during the ceremony.

Although the entire marriage service will not be read, key phrases that will act as cues for different things to happen should be rehearsed. Anyone who has to light a candle, read a poem or sing a solo should run through his or her part. The ushers will review the procedure of seating guests and learn where to tell people to go for a drink of water or how to find the rest rooms.

The Wedding Day

"I take thee to my wedded husband (wife)

to have and to hold from this day forward.

For better or worse

for richer or poorer

in sickness and in health

to love and to cherish til death do us part.

According to God's holy ordinance

and thereto I give thee my troth."

Marriage is the intimate sharing of two lives. A satisfying relationship is one in which neither partner is overpowered or absorbed in the life of the other. Marriage requires periods of aloneness, so the individuality of each can continue to be distinctive and deepen. Each partner is the guardian of the other's solitude. To affirm the distance between is to acknowledge the dignity and friendship which gives life to the marriage.. The wedding ceremony commemorates the bride and groom's commitment to share their journey, and it provides an opportunity for relatives and friends to renew their own vows and emotionally support the loving couple.

A Few Ideas for the Ceremony

American Indian Wedding Prayer

Great Spirit, whose touch moves the winds, and whose breath gives song to the earth, come sit with me, so I can give thanks for the sharing gifts of another and receive Your vision for my life.

Teach me to seek and perceive myself within the medicine wheel of my partner, my people...the spirit of the universe, and give me the courage to know the great harmony with every living thing that all creatures share.

Make my mind willing and my ears keen to hear your voice. Teach me the things of the heart through touching, so that I may overcome my loneliness, and become all that I am.

Help each of us to be as a gift to each other. Perceiving of ourselves as we are, let us see through Your eyes.

A Traditional Wedding Prayer

Lord, we humbly ask you to bless our marriage. Having drawn close through mutual affection, common values and goals, we ask for your help and guidance.

We are grateful for the love that has reduced our selfishness, expanded our hearts and made our lives more meaningful. Help us to continue to grow in understanding through acts of kindness.

Teach us to communicate our true feelings with love and caring, so we can gain knowledge of ourselves and one another. Inspire our affection, so it overflows into the lives of others.

Fill us with gratitude, so our love is sustained through times of doubt, and teach us to follow our heart's desire, and become all that we can be.

Some Ideas

- *I pledge to share my life openly with you.*
- *I vow to fulfill my human potential and support you in fulfilling yours.*
- *I want to live with you just as you are.*
- *I promise to give you the space to be and grow.*
- *I promise to be faithful to our commitment to share our lives.*
- *I promise to invest in our friendship and communicate my feelings with love.*
- *I vow to live within our means, and seek elegance instead of luxury; refinement rather than fashion and wealth instead of riches.*
- *I promise to be kind, and when I am wrong admit it.*
- *I promise to be affectionate, and when I am right, be kind.*
- *My commitment to you is for all of my life.*

Love is a power that liberates the potential for morality. It has nothing to do with finding the right person and everything to do with generating the conditions under which one expresses his or her real self. Marriage requires this kind of environment: where two people make a passionate effort to become the embodiment of truth.

— Philosophy of the Buddha

The Reception

The Receiving Line

For a smaller reception, consider having your receiving line at the ceremony site. That way, you can greet all your guests personally, including the ones that won't be coming to the reception. The photographer can take some beautiful pictures while you are receiving your guests.

A larger reception usually begins with a receiving line that consists of the mother and father of the bride, mother and father of the groom, the bride and groom and the bridal attendants. Go over the guest list with your groom the night before if you are not sure of people's names. Place the guest book, pictures and albums near the receiving line.

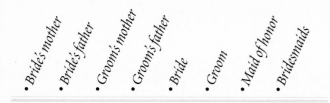

BEGINNING   END

Seating

Sit down luncheons or dinner receptions require a seating plan. If your buffet is a full meal, you will also need to plan the seating. Select a centrally located table for the bridal party. Reserve it with a decorative sign. Plan a special table for both your parents and your officiant (and spouse), if they are not seated at the bridal table.

Placecards are traditionally placed on the bridal table, but they are optional at the other tables. If you are using placecards on all the tables, write the names on both sides of the cards.

SEATING OPTIONS AT THE BRIDAL TABLE

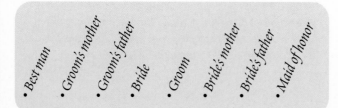

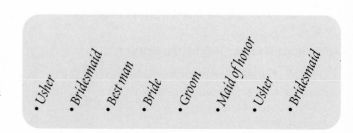

The Reception Procedure

After about an hour of dancing, refreshments, hors'doeuvres, mingling and music, dinner or lunch is served or the buffet is announced. Once everyone is seated and eating, the best man toasts the bride and groom.

The best man honors the newlyweds with the first toast at the beginning of the meal, after the meal is finished and before the cake cutting. At the end of all the toasting, he reads aloud the telegrams and congratulatory letters.

The Order of Dancing

The groom escorts his bride to the dance floor, and they have their first dance to their favorite song. The bride's father cuts in to dance with the bride, while the groom dances with his mother-in-law. (If the parents are divorced, and it is awkward to choose, everyone can be invited to dance midway through the couple's first dance.)

The bride dances with the father of the groom, while the groom dances with his mother. Then, the bride dances with the best man, while the groom dances with the honor attendant. The band leader or "DJ" invites everyone to dance. Ushers dance with bridesmaids and the mothers of the wedding couple.

Some couples prefer to wait until dinner is finished, and the cake is cut and served before dancing. In a larger reception, dancing starts at the end of the reception line. It gives people something to do. The order of dancing can begin any time.

Surprise your guests by taking ballroom dance lessons. Learn to waltz, cha-cha, fox-trot and swing. Keep it your secret, and watch the surprised faces as you both strut your stuff. Your guests will loosen up if they see you having fun on the dance floor.

Cutting the Wedding Cake

The groom places his right hand over hers, and together they cut the first slice. Then, they offer each other first bites. Feeding each other is symbolic of nurturing, caring and tenderness. The groom serves his in-laws first, and the bride does the same. The remainder of the cake is cut and served by the catering staff, family or friends.

Tossing the Bouquet and Garter

The bride throws her bouquet, and the groom throws her garter during the last half hour of the reception. Have someone ask all the single ladies to gather for the throwing of the bouquet. At this time, the groom removes the bride's garter, and tosses it to a gathered group of single men. Have your photographer take pictures of the two lucky people with the bridal couple.

The Honeymoon Exit

Say your good-byes to family and friends before slipping away to change. When you and your groom leave, the main attraction is on hold, so change quickly. Don't leave your guests waiting. Arrange to have someone pass out tossing material, so your departure can be under a shower of rice, birdseed, flower petals, confetti or golden stars.

RIBBONS AND BOWS

Simple Bow

You can vary the simple bow by adding extra loops and tails before you wire the center together; staggering the length of the tails or exaggerating the width of the bow. Add some decorative detail to the center with a glue gun or floral wire.

1 Cross ribbon ends making the tails as long and the bow as wide as you want. Where the ribbon crosses is the center of the bow.

2 Bring the center to the crossed tails and pinch the bow together. Secure the center with a small piece of floral wire or ribbon.

3 Cut the tails at an angle or in points to finish off the look of the bow.

Wiring Stems

By wiring the stems together, the flowers and ferns are held securely in place. It also adds flexibility to the "handle" of the project allowing it to bend.

1 Loosely wrap the wire around the full length of the stems.

2 Cut stems even across the bottom before taping.

Taping Wired Stems

1 Wrap a piece of floral tape around the top of the wire, and press in place.

2 Turn the stems while stretching and pulling the tape in a downward angle. The tape should be tightly wrapped around the wired stems without buckles or gaps.

Wrapping Stems with Ribbon

1 Hot glue the end of the ribbon 1" from the bottom of the stems.

2 Pull the ribbon around the bottom of the stems, and wrap carefully up the length of the stems. Hot glue at the top to secure, and trim off any extra ribbon.

Note: To add tails to the wrapped stems, hot glue ends of ribbons to ends of stems before wrapping the stems with ribbon.

FLORIST BOW

These directions describe how to make a bow using three yards of ribbon. By adjusting the streamer length, loop size and number of loops, the same technique can be used to make any size bow.

1 Measure about 14" for the first tail. With the right side of the ribbon facing out, make a loop on one side using 8-9" of ribbon. Pinch the ribbon together, and hold it with your thumb and forefinger.

2 Twist the ribbon so the right side is facing out, and make a loop toward the other side.

3 Repeat the process of twisting the ribbon as you continue to make loops on both sides. Make each set of loops a little smaller than the previous set.

4 To complete the bow, twist the remaining ribbon around your thumb to make the center loop. Adjust the tail so the right side is facing out. Put a piece of wire through the center and twist it at the back of the bow. The wire should be tight enough to secure the bow, but loose enough to adjust the loops.

5 Spread the loops of the bow, and cut the ends of the tails.

LOOPY BOW

1 Make a loop leaving the tail the desired length.

2 Continue making loops, keeping them uniform in size, until the bow is full, and you have enough ribbon to make the remaining tail.

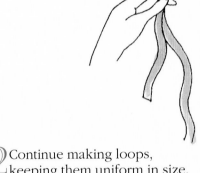

3 Secure the center of the bow with floral wire.

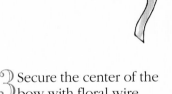

4 Fan out the loops

5 Cut the tails at an angle or in points to finish off the bow.

Create Your Own Decorations and Accessories

"E•Z Bowz" professional bow maker

The E•Z Bow Maker™ comes with a full set of instructions so you can make professional bows every time. A video tape demonstrating this simple bow making tool may also be purchased.

The bow maker consists of a 2" wide, 18" long, wooden base with inches indicated on the top. Two holes for two 8" dowels, to be tapped into place with a hammer, hold the ribbon in place. It allows you to make perfect, beautiful bows from 2" to 16" wide.

The E•Z Bow Maker was designed to make bow making easy! You simply twist the ribbon, and insert it between the dowels. Then loop the ribbon back and forth across the top of the base. Make the loops as wide you wish and add as many loops as you want. Secure the center of the bow with floral wire, and fan out the loops on each side. Lift it from the base.

Purchase your E•Z Bow Maker at your local craft or fabric store or send $19.95 plus $3.50 shipping & handling for the bow maker and video to:
Mark Publishing, 5400 Scotts Valley Dr., Scotts Valley, CA 95066, Phone: (408)438-7668

Make sixteen exciting, different style bows for every occasion.

PINWHEEL BOW

CORSAGE BOW

TAILORED BOW

LAYERED BOW

MUM BOW

PIGGYBACK BOW

TUXEDO BOW

BUTTERFLY BOW

LAYERED BOW WITH TAILS

FLORAL BOW

WREATH BOW

TREE TOP BOW

SWAG BOW

PEW BOW

NESTED BOW

DOUBLE RIBBON BOW

Wedding Wreath I

Materials

- *10" Styrofoam wreath (white)*
- *3 ½ Yards 2" (pattern) wire edge ribbon*
- *3 Floral pins*
- *Floral wire (light weight)*
- *Floral tape (white)*
- *2 Stems plumosus fern*
- *3 Stems (purple) freesia*
- *3 Stems (pink) azalea (or any similar flower)*

Tools

- *Scissors*
- *Low melt glue gun/glue sticks*
- *Wire cutters*

1 Ribbon and floral pins. Attach ribbon to back of wreath with two floral pins, and wrap evenly around entire wreath. Cut ribbon and secure end with third floral pin. Cut a 9" piece of ribbon (set aside). Make a 7" wide, 4 loop Florist bow (page 25) with a center loop and 7" tails. Set the bow aside.

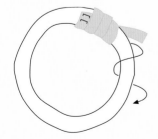

Instructions

2 Remaining materials. Lay the plumosus on a table. Lay the freesia on top of the plumosus. Cut the azaleas into single stems, and arrange them on top of the freesia. (The arrangement is 10" long, not including the stems.) Wire the stems together. (See page 24.) Cut the stems to 3" long. Wrap the wired stems with floral tape.

3 Remaining ribbon and bow. Wrap the stems with the 9" piece of ribbon (see page 24). Hot glue the bow just below the flowers. Hot glue the "bouquet" to the wreath slightly at an angle.

Wedding Wreath II

Materials

- 16" Grapevine wreath
- White spray paint
- 6' (White) dried look rose garland
- 2 Stems (white) anemones (3 flowers each)
- 8 Stems dried (natural) caspia
- 3 Yards (off white) 2½" sheer ribbon
- 2 Pearl sprays

Tools

- Wire cutters
- Floral wire
- Low melt glue gun/glue sticks

1 White paint. Spray wreath lightly, and allow to dry.

Instructions

2 Rose garland. Wire the ends to the wreath at 12:00. Wire the garland at 3:00, 6:00 and 9:00 o'clock. Continue to wire as needed.

3 Ribbon, pearl sprays. Make a 14" wide Florist bow (see page 25) with 6 loops and 12" tails. Hot glue the bow to the top center of the wreath. Glue the pearl sprays to the wreath in-between the loops of the bow.

4 Anemones. Pull the flowers from the stems, and hot glue one flower to the center of the bow. Glue the rest throughout the wreath.

5 Caspia. Break the stems into 6" pieces and insert in between the grapevines all around the wreath.

Door Decoration

Materials

- K2510 Berdestone cherubim
- 1-6' (Pink), open rose garland
- 1-6' (Pink), rosebud garland
- 1-6' (White), rosebud garland

Tools

- Scissors
- Masking tape
- Wire cutters

Instructions

Note: Call Aldik Artificial Flower Company, Inc. for information about Berdestone Products: (805)295-0170

1 Cherubim and open rose garland. Hang the cherubim on your door or wall. Starting with the middle of the garland at the top, tape the garland to the door around the cherubim.

2 Pink and white rosebud garlands. Cut the garlands into 12" pieces and fill in the empty spaces around the open rose garland. Tape to secure. Place a few roses and leaves in the bowl.

Wooden Wedding Arch

Materials

- 1-6' (Pink) open rose garland
- 2-6' (Pink) rosebud garlands
- 1-6' (White) rosebud garland
- 5 Stems (pink) peonies
- 1 Spool 6" (pink) tulle
- 2 Spools 6" (white) tulle

Tools

- Scissors
- Duct tape
- Florist wire

1 Pink rosebud garlands. Wind one garland through the lattice on each side of the arch.

2 Open rose garland. Tape the middle of the garland to the middle of the arch. Use small pieces of tape. Tape the garland across the front of the arch.

Instructions

3 White rosebud garlands. Cut into 6" sections, and wind pieces around the open rose garland on top of the arch. Tape to secure.

4 White tulle. Make two 12" wide, 10 loop Loopy bows (see page 25), with 28" tails. Tape one to the front of the arch in the center and one on top of the arch in back of the garland. Make two 10" wide, 8 loop Loopy bows with 28" tails. Tape one on either side of the arch. Cut the remaining white tulle in half, and drape, tuck and tape, working from the center of the arch down to the side bows.

5 Pink tulle. Make two 12" wide, 10 loop Loopy bows with 28" tails. Tape one on top of the front, white bow and one on the top of the bow on top of the arch. Make two 10" wide, 8 loop Loopy bows with 28" tails, and tape one bow to the middle of each side bow.

6 Peonies. Cut all the stems to 5" long, and tape or wire one flower over each side bow and the remaining flowers on top of the front center, tulle bow. Face them slightly downward.

Note: Arches can be rented at party or wedding supply businesses.

Suggestion: Surround the decorated arch with artificial or fresh trees and arrangements. For an evening or late afternoon wedding, add small lights to the trees.

GUEST BOOK

Materials

- Three ring binder
- 1 Package binder paper
- 1 Yard (white) satin fabric
- 1 Yard ½" wide (white) trim
- 12" X 21" Piece of batting
- 10 Yards (white) braiding
- 1 Yard (white) roses on a ribbon trim
- 1 Yard small string of pearls (knotted)
- ⅔ Yard (white) 4" wide lace
- 2 Pieces 10½" X 9" light weight cardboard

Tools

- Scissors
- Low melt glue gun/glue sticks
- Iron

Instructions

1 White satin and batting. Iron the fabric, and cut a 26" X 16" piece. Lay the fabric, right side down on a table. Lay the batting in the middle, and the open binder on top of the batting. Glue the fabric to the inside of the binder. Cut the inside edges to within ½" of the edge of the binder.

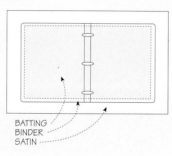

BATTING
BINDER
SATIN

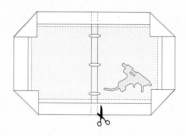

2 Braiding. Cut two 11½" pieces. Glue them inside, on either side of the three rings.

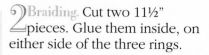
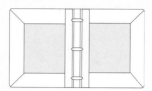

3 All the trim. Cut all the trim, except the lace, in half. Starting from the inside of the binder, glue all the trim in place. See photo for placement.

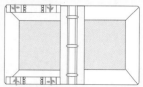

GLUE THE ENDS OF THE TRIM TO THE INSIDE OF THE BINDER AND WRAP AROUND THE FRONT

4 Cardboard and fabric. Cut two pieces of 11" X 14" satin fabric. Iron the pieces. Place a piece of cardboard in the middle of each piece of fabric. Glue the corners first. Then, glue the sides to the cardboard. To finish off the inside of the guest book, hot glue the covered cardboard on the inside front and back covers.

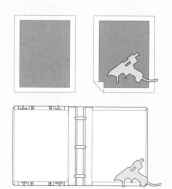

PEW BOW

Materials

- 10 Yards 2½" wide (white) ribbon
- 1½ Yards ⅛" wide (ivory) ribbon
- 1 Stem (white) open rose
- 4 Pearl sprays
- Floral wire

Tools

- Wire cutters
- Scissors

1 Ribbons. Make an 11" wide, 16 loop Loopy bow with 14" and 16" tails (see page 25). Cut the ivory ribbon in half. Using both pieces as one ribbon, tie around the center of the white bow. Cut the ends of the white ribbon in a "V" shape.

Note: Use the stem to anchor the bow to special pews or chairs.

Instructions

2 Rose and pearl sprays. Cut the rose stem to 8" long. Hot glue the rose to the center of the bow in between the loops. Wrap the stems of the pearl sprays around the stem of the rose to secure.

Wedding Topiary

Materials

- 1-10" Styrofoam ball
- 1-12" Styrofoam ball
- 7" Wide 6" tall pedestal vase
- 2 Floral foam (green)
- 2-10" Long 1½" wide branches
- 2 Large packages sphagnum moss
- Floral pins
- Tacky glue
- 1 Spray ivy (12 stems)
- 2 Stems (white) Canterbury bells
- 4 Stems (white) baby's breath
- 3½ Yards 2½" wide sheer (off white) ribbon

Tools

- Low melt glue gun/glue sticks
- Wire cutters
- Scissors

Instructions

1. **Styrofoam balls, moss, tacky glue and branches.** Cover balls with tacky glue and adhere moss to balls. Insert branches 2"-3" into the centers of the balls. Remove branches, and fill holes with hot glue. Replace branches in holes and set aside.

2. **Floral foam and moss.** Cut one foam to fit vase snugly. Hot glue to secure. Use extra foam to fill in pot. Insert balls and branches into center of foam. Hot glue to secure. Cover foam with moss, and secure with floral pins.

3. **Ivy.** Cut the stems from the ivy, and wrap around the balls in a random pattern. Secure with floral pins.

4. **Ribbon.** Make a 12" wide, 8 loop Florist bow (see page 25), with 18" tails. Hot glue bow to top of topiary. Tack down the tails of the bow in graceful curves with floral pins, or use hot glue.

5. **Canterbury bells.** Cut into 2" to 3" sections, and floral pin the pieces to topiary.

6. **Baby's breath.** Cut into single 6" stems, and insert into the foam around the top of the container.

Suggestion: Set your topiary tree next to the guest book.

BRIDAL TABLE ARRANGEMENT

Materials

- 3" High, 5" wide round vase
- 3½ Yards 2" wide, wire edge ribbon
- 1 Floral foam (green)
- 4 Stems calla lilies
- 8 Stems (green/white) plumes
- 3 Stems (white) delphinium
- 2 Stems (white) liatris
- 7 Stems plumosus fern
- 2 Stems (white) rosebuds
- 1 Stem (white) poppy
- 4 Stems (white) baby's breath

Tools

- Wire cutters
- Low melt glue gun/glue sticks
- Floral wire

1 Foam. Cut foam to fit snugly and extend 2" above rim of vase. Hot glue to bottom of container.

LET FOAM EXTEND 2"

2 Ribbon. Make a 12" wide, 10 loop Loopy bow (see page 25), with 18" tails. Fan out the loops, and hot glue to the center of the foam. Tuck the tails into the side of the vase to cover the foam.

Instructions

3 Calla lilies. Cut stems to 9", 9", 7",7" tall. Measure from top of flowers. Insert in between loops of bows.

4 Plumes. Cut six stems to 15" tall and two stems to 10" tall.

STEPS 4-10 SHOW TOP VIEW OF ARRANGEMANT AND POSITION OF FLOWERS

5 Liatris. Both are 14" tall.

6 Delphinium. Cut two to 17" tall and one to 12" tall.

7 Rosebuds. Cut each stem into two 11" stems.

8 Poppy. Cut to 12" tall.

9 Baby's breath. Cut to 12" tall.

10 Plumosus fern. Use various lengths throughout arrangement.

Note: Substitute with similar flowers if those listed are not available.

Wedding Arrangement

Materials

- 1 4" Tall (white) vase
- 3 Floral foam (green)
- 3⅓ Yards 2½" wide (sheer) ribbon
- 3 Stems (white) open roses
- 6 Stems (white) rosebuds
- 6 Stems (white) sweet williams
- 6 Stems (white) mums
- 3 Stems (white) mini roses
- 2 Stems (white) ranunculus
- 2 Stems (white) dogwood
- 6 Stems (white) baby's breath
- 1 Bush (green) ivy (15 stems)

Tools

- Wire cutters
- Floral wire

1 Floral foam. Insert one full block of foam into vase. Wedge second foam across top of first foam. Fill in with pieces of third foam until vase is filled with foam.

2 Ivy. Insert bush into center of foam. Arrange stems.

Instructions

3 Open roses. Cut stems to 13", 13" and 15".

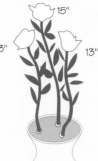

4 Rose buds. Cut stems to 18", 18" 22", 22", 24" and 26" tall.

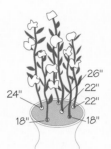

5 Mums. All stems are 18" long.

6 Sweet williams. All stems are 18" long.

7 Mini roses. All stems are 17" long.

8 Ranunculus. All are 10" long.

9 Dogwood. All are 10" long.

10 Baby's breath. All stems are 16" long.

11 Ribbon. Make a 12" wide, 4 loop Loopy with 14" tails (see page 25). Hot glue to front edge of arrangement.

Note: Substitute with similar flowers if those listed are not available.

TABLE CENTERPIECE I

Materials

- 6" Wide, 3" tall round vase
- 1 Floral foam (green)
- 5 Yards, 3" wide lace ribbon
- 3 Stems (burgundy) roses (3 flowers each)
- 2 Stems (blue) lavender (3 flowers each)
- 3 Stems (multi-colored) field flowers
- 6 Stems plumosus fern
- Floral wire

Tools

- Low melt glue gun/glue sticks
- Wire cutters
- Scissors

Instructions

1 Floral foam and vase. Wedge the foam snugly into vase.

2 Ribbon. Cut ribbon in half, and make two 8" wide, 4 loop Loopy bows (see page 25), with 11" tails. Hot glue the bows side by side to the top of the foam. Tuck the tails inside the vase to add extra loops and cover the foam..

Note: Insert all the flowers in between the loops of the bow.

3 Lavender. Cut into 6 single 7" stems

4 Roses. Cut into 9 single 7" stems.

5 Field flowers. Cut flowers apart into three 7" stems each.

6 Plumosus fern. Use available lengths, and insert as shown.

TABLE CENTERPIECE II

Materials

- 6" Twig wreath
- White spray paint
- Florist wire (light weight)
- 4 Stems (peach) mini delphiniums
- 2 Stems (pink) rosebuds
- 2 Stems (burgundy) rosebuds
- 3 Stems (white) baby's breath
- 2 Stems (purple) star jasmine
- 1 (pink) 10" tall candle

Tools

- Wire cutters
- Low melt glue gun/glue sticks

1 Spray paint. Spray wreath, and allow to dry.

2 Delphiniums. Cut two stems at the base of the flowers, and wire them together in a circle. Hot glue to top of wreath. Pull the flowers from the remaining delphiniums, and fill in the circle of flowers. (Turn the wreath upside down to cover the lower edge.)

Instructions

3 Rosebuds. Pull the flowers from the stems, and hot glue randomly around the top of the wreath.

4 Star jasmine. Cut into 2" sections with 3-4 flowers each, and hot glue in between other flowers.

5 Baby's breath and candle. Cut each stem into three 2" sections, and hot glue throughout flowers. Add the candle.

TABLE CENTERPIECE III

Materials

- 11" Tall pedestal vase
- 1 Stem (peach) open rose
- 3 Stems (white) baby's breath
- 2 Stems (pink) field flowers
- 2 Yards (peach) ¾" wide ribbon
- Floral wire (light weight)
- 2" X 2½" Piece of floral foam

Tools

- Wire cutters
- Low melt glue gun/glue sticks

1 Floral foam, vase and flowers. Hot glue the foam in the vase. Cut all the stems of the flowers to 3½" long. Measure from the top of the flowers. Insert the rose fully into the center of the foam. Insert the baby's breath and field flowers around the rose.

Instructions

2 Ribbon. Make a 10" wide, 4 loop Loopy bow with 12" to 14" tails (see page 25). Hot glue the bow to the edge of the vase.

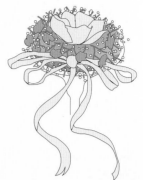

Optional: Glue a border of 1" lace around the edge of the vase before adding the flowers.

WEDDING CAKE DECORATION

Materials

- *Plastic cake top*
- *Cherub (or bride and groom)*
- *1 Stem (white) large rose*
- *1 Stem (pink) medium rose*
- *Small pieces of (white and purple) lilac*
- *⅓ Yard (pink) dotted netting*
- *1 Yard (pink) 2" wide sheer ribbon*

Tools

- *Wire cutter*
- *Scissors*
- *Low melt glue gun/glue sticks*

Instructions

3 Netting. Cut a 6" X 36" strip of netting, and make a 12" wide 2 loop Loopy bow with 6" tails (see page 25). Hot glue to plastic cake top in back of flowers.

4 Sheer ribbon. Glue the middle of the ribbon (streamers) to the cake top under the lilacs.

1 Cherub. Hot glue the cherub to the plastic cake top.

2 Flowers and leaves. Cut the white rose to 5" and the rest of the flowers to 3". Glue the pink rose left of the cherub, the lilac pieces to the right and the white rose in back. Hot glue leaves around the flowers and cherub.

Punch Bowl Wreath

Materials

- 18" Grapevine wreath
- White spray paint
- Floral wire (light weight)
- 1-6' Long (pink) open rose garland
- 4 Stems (peach) baby's breath
- 6 Stems (purple) dried baby's breath

Tools

- Wire cutters

Instructions

1 Spray paint. Spray wreath, and allow to dry.

2 Garland. Wire garland to top of wreath. Secure at 12:00, 3:00, 6:00 and 9:00 o'clock.

3 White baby's breath. Cut each stem into three single 5-6" stems, and insert into the branches of the wreath in between the roses.

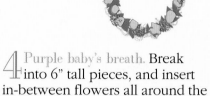

4 Purple baby's breath. Break into 6" tall pieces, and insert in-between flowers all around the wreath.

Decorated Bread Basket

Materials

- *17" Long 6" high, 10" wide (white) rectangular basket with handle*
- *4 Yards (gold) 2" wide sheer wired ribbon*
- *2 Stems (burgundy) hydrangeas*
- *2 Stems (burgundy) rosebuds*
- *3 Stems (pink) baby's breath*
- *Floral wire (light weight)*

Tools

- *Wire cutters*
- *Low melt glue gun/glue sticks*
- *Scissors*

1 Ribbon. Cut 1 1/2 yards to wrap handle. Glue one end of the ribbon to the inside of the handle, and wrap the handle tightly. Glue end to secure. Make a 10" wide, 4 loop Loopy bow (see page 25) with 24" tails. Glue bow on outside of handle.

Note: Arrange the tails in graceful curves around the basket.

2 Hydrangeas. Cut the stems to 1" long, and glue one in the center of the bow and one underneath the loops.

Instructions

3 Roses. Cut the stems to 4" tall, and hot glue three roses above the hydrangeas, on the handle, three to the left and three to the right of the hydrangeas, under the loops of the bow. Add three more to the inside handle on the opposite side of the basket. Intersperse with leaves.

4 Baby's breath. Cut each stem into three sections, and glue throughout flowers and bow.

Materials

CHAMPAGNE BOTTLE

- 2 Yards, 2" wide (gold) sheer, wired ribbon
- 1 Silk rose
- Florist wire (light weight)

CAKE KNIFE

- 2 Yards (cream) ¼" wide ribbon
- 1½ Yards (white) ⅛" wide ribbon
- 1 Silk rose

BRIDE & GROOM GLASSES

- 2-8" Wide net circles
- 2 Yards ½" wide (cream) ribbon
- 1 Yard ⅛" wide (white) ribbon
- 2 Silk roses

Tools

- Scissors
- Low melt glue gun/glue sticks

BRIDE & GROOM GLASSES

1 Net circles, white and cream ribbon and roses. Fold the circles in half and then in half again. Cut ½" off the bottom point. Slip the circles around the bottoms of the glasses. Cut the white ribbon in half, and tie the ribbons around the tops of the circles to hold them in place. Make shoelace bows using two pieces of cream ribbon for each glass. Hot glue to center of white ribbon. Glue roses to the centers of the bows.

Instructions

CAKE KNIFE

1 Both ribbons. Cut the ribbons in half, and (holding all the ribbons as one) tie them in a knot around the top of the handle.

2 Rose. Hot glue the rose over the knotted ribbons.

CHAMPAGNE BOTTLE

1 Ribbon. Cut a 24" piece of ribbon, and tie it around the neck of the bottle. Make an 8" wide, 4 loop Florist bow (see page 25), with a button loop and 10" tails. Hot glue the bow to the knotted ribbon on the bottle.

2 Rose. Hot glue the rose under the button loop.

Favors

Materials

GOLDEN POTPOURRI

- 9" (Gold) 3" wide, sheer wire ribbon
- 2 Yards ⅛" wide (gold) ribbon
- Small amount of potpourri

SOPHISTICATED FAVOR

- 8" (White) 2" wide, opaque wire ribbon
- 5 Jordan almonds
- 1 Silk rose

VICTORIAN FAVOR

- 8" Printed mesh ribbon 3" wide
- 5 Jordan almonds
- 1 Silk rose

TRADITIONAL TULLE FAVOR

- 18" Square of (pink) tulle
- 18" Square of (white dotted) tulle
- 12" Of ⅛" wide (white) ribbon
- Small sprig of tiny flowers

Tools

- Scissors
- Low melt glue gun/glue sticks

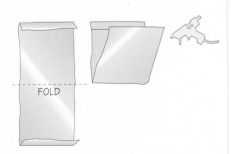

SEE INSTRUCTIONS FOR GOLDEN POTPOURRI ABOVE.

Instructions

GOLDEN POTPOURRI

All materials. Fold the ends of the 3" wide ribbon over 1/2". Fold ribbon in half, and glue the sides together. Put the potpourri inside, and glue the top closed. Cut the narrow ribbon in half, and, using the ribbons as one, wrap like a present with a simple bow on top.

SOPHISTICATED FAVOR

All materials. Fold ribbon in half, and glue sides together. Fill with almonds. Fold ends at angles and glue point down to secure. Glue rose over the point of the ribbon.

VICTORIAN FAVOR

All materials. Fold ribbon in half, and glue the sides. Fill with almonds. Glue the ends. Cut an interesting shape. Glue rosebud at the top.

TRADITIONAL TULLE FAVOR

All materials. Lay the pink tulle on top of the white tulle. Put the almonds in the center. Gather the tulle, and tie a knot and a bow. Glue flowers on top of the bow.

PLACECARDS

Materials

- Water colors (any selection plus white)
- Kitchen sponge (small)
- Watercolor paper (16"X18")
- Rubber cement
- Gold foil
- ½" Wide lace (optional)
- Rubber cement pick up (eraser)
- ⅛" Wide (Ivory) ribbon
- ¾" Wide Satin roses

Tools

- Scissors
- Ruler
- Spoon
- Pencil

Instructions

1 Paper, sponge and paints. Soak the sponge with water and moisten the paper thoroughly. Cut the sponge in half. Dot different colors of paint on the sponge, and smear it all over the paper. Play with the surface and create textures. Add more colors or leave as is. Allow to dry completely.

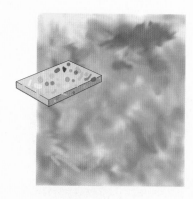

2 Rubber cement and gold foil. Apply streaks of rubber cement to the dry painting in random patterns. Apply rubber cement to the front of the gold foil. Allow to dry thoroughly. Lay the gold foil face down, on top of the rubber cement on the painting and rub the gold backing with the back of a spoon. Streaks of gold will adhere to the painting.

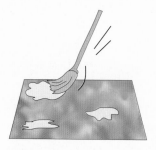

3 Rubber cement pick up. Carefully clean up the excess rubber cement from your painting. Draw a grid over the painting, and cut out your placecards. Each card is 4" X 6". Use the same technique to make your bridal table sign. Use hot glue to add lace to the sign (optional).

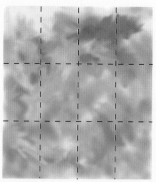

4 Adding the names. Make a pencil grid on a fresh sheet of watercolor paper. The names are 1½" X ½". Write in the names of your guests. Rubber cement the back of the paper, and add a small touch of rubber cement to the front of your cards. Allow to dry. Cut out the names and stick them on the placecards. Make a heart and add your message to the bridal table sign.

5 Ribbon and roses. Cut 5" pieces of ribbon. Fold them over, and glue them to the right hand corners of the cards. Cut the stems from the roses, and hot glue them on top of the ribbons where they cross.

BRIDE'S GARTER

Materials

- 1 Lace fringed garter
- 1 (Pink) rose bud
- Small amount of tiny flowers
- Small pieces of plumosus fern
- 24" (White) 2" wide sheer ribbon with gold edge
- Floral wire (light weight)

Tools

- Low melt glue gun/glue sticks
- Wire cutters

Instructions

1 Ribbon. Make a 5" wide, 2 loop simple bow with 8-10" tails. Secure the center with floral wire.

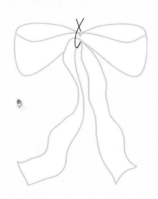

2 Flowers and fern. Glue rose to center of bow. Add small pieces of fern and flowers around rose. Glue bow to garter.

BRIDAL COMB

Materials

- 2 Satin roses 3" wide
- 4 Pearl sprays
- 6 Satin roses (small)
- 1½ Yards ⅛" wide (white) ribbon
- 1 Plastic comb 3"

Tools

- Scissors
- Low melt glue gun/glue sticks

Instructions

1 Ribbon. Cut the ribbon in half, and make a simple 7" wide shoe lace bow using both the ribbon pieces. Glue to the center of the comb.

2 3" Roses. Cut the stems to ½" long, and glue one on either side of the comb, in the center.

3 Small roses. Cut the stems to 1½" long, and glue around roses on both sides.

4 Pearl sprays. Cut the stems to 1" long, and glue two on each side of the big roses.

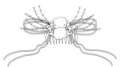

White Bridal Bouquet

Materials

- 5 Stems open (white) roses
- 8 Stems (white) baby's breath
- 3 Stems (white) plumes
- 1 Stem (white) mini delphinium
- 6 Stems (green) plumosus
- 4½ Yards striped 2" wide (white) ribbon
- Floral wire (light weight)
- Floral tape (white)

Tools

- Wire cutters
- Scissors
- Low melt glue gun/glue sticks

Note: If the bouquet needs another flower or two to fill an open space, hot glue flower heads directly onto the bouquet. Also, if the bottom fern does not reach the end of the bouquet, hot glue a piece on the bottom of the bouquet to extend beyond the flowers.

Instructions

1 3 Stems plumosus, 2 stems plumes, 4 stems baby's breath, delphinium. Lay the plumosus on a table. Lay the plumes, baby's breath and delphinium on top of the fern.

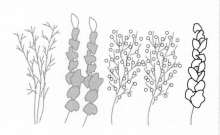

2 2 Stems plumosus, 1 plume, 4 stems baby's breath. Layer the flowers and ferns in the same way graduating the layers. (The arrangement is 18" long, not including the stems.)

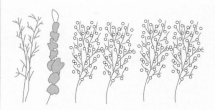

3 Roses. Layer the roses on top of the arrangement. Secure 10" of the stems with florist wire. Cut the stems even at the bottom. Wrap the stems with floral tape (see page 24).

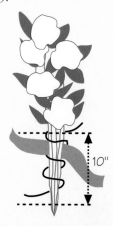

4 Ribbon. Cut off a 16" and a 25" piece of ribbon. Wrap the stem with the 25" piece of ribbon, and tie the 16" piece around the top of the stems for extra tails. (See page 24). Make a 12" wide, loop Florist bow (see page 25), with 18" tails. Hot glue the bow to the top of the stems under the flowers.

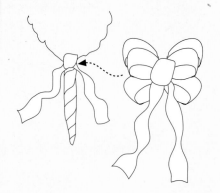

BRIDAL VEILS

Materials

DUCHESS

- *2" Wide 8½" long satin covered headband*
- *3" Comb*
- *Finger tip double tier veil*
- *6 Single roses with pearl tip centers (3" diameter)*
- *3 Clusters of small satin and organza flowers*
- *3 Pkgs. circle pearls (9.5" long)*
- *5 Pkgs. pearl loops (1" diameter)*
- *2 Pkgs. pearl loops (2" diameter)*
- *2 Pkgs. Glittering balls*

Tools

- *Low melt glue gun/glue sticks*
- *Wire cutters*
- *Ruler*

Note: This headband is a Lotus, California, Inc. design and can be purchased as a kit with instructions in the wedding department at your craft store.

Instructions

1 Headband, veil and comb. Shape the headband to fit the bride's head. Hot glue comb (or sew) comb to headband. Sew the veil to the center of the headband, or secure it with hot glue.

2 Roses and organza flowers. Cut the stems from the roses, and hot glue them end to end on top of the veil, across the entire headband. Cut the flower stems to ½", and hot glue four around each rose.

3 Circle pearls & 1" pearl loops. Cut the circle pearl stems to 1" long. Hot glue three stems around each rose. Bend them into graceful shapes. Cut the loop stems to ½", and hot glue four around each rose

4 2" Pearl loops and glittering balls. Cut the pearl loop stems to ½", and hot glue two loops around each rose. Cut the glittering ball stems to 1", and hot glue them 4" apart across the top of the headband.

Materials

COUNTESS

- 2" Wide satin headband
- 3" Comb
- Finger tip double tier veil
- 1 Pouff veil
- 5 Sprays satin & organza flowers with pearls (6 flowers each)
- 5 Clusters rose buds with pearls (2" diameter)
- 2 Sprays rosebuds with lily of the valley (6" long)

Tools

- Wire cutters
- Low melt glue gun/glue sticks

1 Headpiece, comb & pouff veil. Shape the headpiece to fit the bride's head, and hot glue or stitch the comb to the headband. Hot glue or stitch the pouff veil to the center of the headpiece.

2 Bridal veil. Glue or stitch the longer veil to the center of the headpiece on top of the pouff veil.

Instructions

3 Satin & organza flowers. Hot glue two sprays on each side facing outward and extending 1" beyond the headband. Cut the last spray into six, single clusters, with 2" stems, and hot glue on top of the center stems.

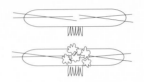

4 Rosebud clusters. Cut the stems to 1" long, and hot glue in the open spaces.

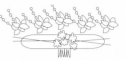

5 Rose & lily of the valley sprays. Hot glue one spray at each end of the band under the flowers.

BRIDAL HAT

Materials

- Victorian lace hat
- 3 Yards 2" wide (white) striped ribbon
- 6 Stems (peach) micro roses

Tools

- Wire cutters
- Low melt glue gun/glue sticks

Note: Hat may be purchased at local craft stores.

Instructions

1. **Ribbon.** Make a 7" wide, 6 loop Florist bow (see page 25) with 16" and 18" tails. Hot glue the bow to the center of the back.

2. **Roses.** Cut the roses into 6" long sections of 5 roses each, and hot glue to center of bow and under the loops on either side of the bow.

54

PEACH WEDDING BOUQUET

Materials

- 3 Stems (peach) Canterbury bells
- 3 Stems (peach) baby's breath
- 2 Stems (white) baby's breath
- 1 Stem (purple) mini daisies
- 1 Stem (peach) open rose
- 3 Stems plumosus fern
- 4½ Yards 1¾" wide (peach) wire ribbon
- Floral wire (light weight)
- Floral tape (white)

Tools

- Scissors
- Wire cutters

1 Plumosus, mini daisies, 2 stems Canterbury bells, peach baby's breath, rose. Lay the fern on a table and layer the daisies, Canterbury bells, baby's breath and rose. Graduate the arrangement to extend to 18" long (not including the stems) Wire 7" of the stems together. Cut the remaining stems even at the bottom.

Note: If the plumosus is not long enough to extend beyond the flowers, glue a piece to the back of the bouquet when the arrangement is complete.

Instructions

2 Remaining Canterbury bell and white baby's breath. Pull the blooms from the Canterbury bells, and glue them to the top of the bouquet and beneath the rose. Cut small sections of baby's breath, and glue throughout the bouquet.

3 Ribbon and floral tape. Cut off a 20" piece of ribbon, and wrap the stems (see page 24). Make a 9" wide, 8 loop Florist bow (see page 25) with 16" tails. Hot glue the bow close to the bottom flowers.

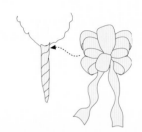

BRIDAL GARLAND & POSIE

Materials

GARLAND

- 6 Stems (peach) mini larkspur
- 2 Sprays (pink) azalea
- 1 Stem (peach) syringa
- 2 Stems (white) rose buds (small)
- 3 Stems (white) baby's breath
- 5 Yards 6" wide (pink) tulle
- 2 Yards 1½" wide (pink) sheer ribbon

Tools

- Floral wire
- Wire cutters
- Scissors
- Low melt glue gun/glue sticks

1 Larkspur. Cut stems from three larkspur, and wire together to form a 25" circle. Remove blossoms from the remaining larkspur, and hot glue throughout garland.

2 Azaleas and roses. Pull the flower heads from the roses and hot glue them in-between the larkspur. Cut the azaleas from the stems and do the same.

3 Syringa and baby's breath. Cut the stems into small 3" clusters, and glue throughout garland.

4 Tulle and ribbons. Using the tulle, make a 10" wide, 8 loop, Loopy bow (see page 25) with 16" tails. Cut the ivory and the sheer ribbon into two slightly uneven pieces each. Wire the sheer and the ivory ribbon together in the middle, and hot glue them to the center of the tulle bow. Hot glue the tulle bow to the back of the garland in the middle of the flowers.

Materials

POSIE

- Plastic posie and lace holder with floral foam and handle
- 3 Stems (peach) open roses
- 4 Sprays (peach) micro roses
- 4 Stems (pink) rosebuds
- 2 Stems (white) baby's breath
- 5 Pearl sprays
- 1½ Yards (pink) 1½" wide wire ribbon
- 1½ Yards (peach) 1½" wide wire ribbon
- 2 Yards (white) ⅛" ribbon

Tools

- Wire cutters
- Low melt glue gun/glue sticks

1 Open roses. All roses are 6" tall.

TOP VIEW SHOWING POSITION OF FLOWERS (INSTRUCTIONS 1-5)

2 Micro roses. Cut into sections of five roses each. All are 6" tall

3 Pink rosebuds. Cut each spray into three sections. All are 6" tall.

4 Baby's breath. Cut each spray into three sections. All are 6" tall.

5 Pearl sprays. Cut an inch from the stems, and glue them into the flowers.

6 Ribbons. Using the pink and peach ribbons, make two 9" wide, 2 loop Loopy bows with 10" and 13" tails (see page 25). Wire together. Hot glue the center of the ⅛" ribbon to the edge of the plastic holder, and hot glue the layered bow on top of the ⅛" ribbon. Cut the tails in "V's".

56

Maid of Honor Headpiece & Bouquet

Materials

Headpiece

- 3" comb
- 2½ Yards 1½" wide (pink) wire edge ribbon
- 1 Stem (pink) open rose (medium size)
- Few pieces of tiny flowers
- Few small rose leaves
- Floral wire (light weight)

Tools

- Wire cutters
- Scissors
- Low melt glue gun/glue sticks

1 **Ribbon and comb.** Make a 7" wide, 10 loop Florist bow with 6" tails. Omit the center loop (see page 25). Glue the bow to the center of the comb.

2 **Rose, leaves and tiny flowers.** Cut the rose stem as short as possible, and hot glue to the center of the bow. Hot glue the leaves and tiny flowers around the rose and in-between the loops of the bow.

Materials

Bouquet

- 1 Stem (white) liatris
- 2 Stems (peach) syringa
- 1 Stem (pink) wild rose
- 2 Stems (pink) poppies
- 2 Stems (burgundy) mini daisies
- 5 Stems plumosus fern
- 1 Stem (peach) large open rose
- 2 Stems (white) jasmine
- 4 Yards (pink) 1½" wide, wire edge ribbon
- Floral wire (light weight)
- Floral tape (white)

Tools

- Wire cutter
- Low melt glue gun/glue sticks
- Scissors

1 **All the flowers, fern and floral wire.** Lay long stems of fern on a table. Lay the liatris, syringa, mini daisies, poppies, wild rose, jasmine and large open rose in a graduated pattern on top of the fern (arrangement is 18" long, not including the stems). Wire the stems together close to the bottom flowers. Cut the stems to 9" long.

2 **Ribbon and tape.** Tape the stems tightly with floral tape. Cut off a 22" piece of ribbon, and wrap the stems (see page 24). Make an 11" wide, 8 loop Florist bow with 18" tails (see page 25). Hot glue the bow under the flowers at the top of the stems.

Maid of Honor Hat

Materials

- 15" (pink) hat
- 1 Stem (peach) open rose
- 1 Stem (purple) lilac
- 1 Stem (pink) small rose
- 1 Stem (purple) hydrangea
- 5 Stems (pink) small rosebuds
- Floral wire (light weight)
- 1 Yard (pink) dotted netting
- 2 Yards (or 22" X 72") (pink) netting
- 1½ Yards (pink) sheer 2" ribbon

Tools

- Wire cutters
- Scissors
- Low melt glue gun/glue sticks

1 Netting. Cut a 22" X 72" strip of plain netting. Wire six equal gathered sections, and glue to hat at even intervals. Cut a 5" X 36" strip of dotted netting, and make a 9" wide, 2 loop Loopy bow with 9" tails (see page 25). Set aside.

2 Hydrangeas and rosebuds. Cut six hydrangea flowerettes, and glue one over each of the glued down puffs. Add one rosebud to each hydrangea flowerette.

Instructions

3 Sheer ribbon and dotted bow. Make a 7" wide 2 loop Loopy bow with 10" tails. Wire the sheer bow to the dotted bow, and hot glue to the center back of the hat.

4 Open rose, lilac and small roses. Cut the stems to 1" long , and glue the open rose to the top of the ribbon. Glue the lilac and roses around the open rose under the ribbon.

FLOWER GIRL HEADBAND & BASKET

Materials

BASKET

- 5" Wide, 5" tall, round (white) basket with handle
- ⅔ Yard double (white) lace
- 6 Sprays (pink) fabric flowers
- 1 Yard (pink) 2" wide, wire edge ribbon
- 3 Yards (white) ⅛" wide ribbon
- 14" Square piece of netting to line the basket
- Potpourri (or flower petals) to fill basket
- Floral wire (light weight)

Tools

- Scissors
- Wire cutters
- Low melt glue gun/glue sticks

1 Pink ribbon. Glue one end to the inside of the handle. Wrap the handle tightly with the ribbon and secure with glue at the other end.

2 Netting. Cut a 14" square piece of netting. Fit it inside the basket. Hot glue the edges of the basket, and press the netting to the rim to secure. Cut off the excess netting around the basket edge.

3 Lace. Hot glue the lace under the lip of the basket.

4 Pink flowers. Cut off the stems, and hot glue the flowers around the edge of the basket. Set aside two single flowers.

5 Ribbon. Cut the ribbon in thirds. Make a simple 2 loop, 4" wide bow with uneven tails. Secure the center with florist wire, and hot glue it to the handle of the basket. Glue the two pink flowers over the center of the bow.

6 Potpourri. Fill the basket with potpourri.

Materials

HEADBAND

- (Pink) Satin headband
- 5 Sprays (pink) fabric flowers
- 1 Pkg (white) tiny silk roses

Tools

- Wire cutters
- Low melt glue gun/glue sticks

1 Pink flowers and headband. Cut the stems of the pink flowers to ½". Hot glue across top of headband.

2 Roses. Cut the stems to ¾" tall, and hot glue throughout the pink flowers.

61

Materials

GARLAND

- 3 Stems (pink) mini delphinium
- 1 Stem (pink) open rose
- 1 Stem (purple) hydrangea
- 1 Stem (white) snowball
- 1½ Yards (green) 2" sheer ribbon
- 1½ Yards (white) 2" sheer ribbon
- 1 Yard (pink) 2" sheer ribbon
- Florist wire (light weight)

Tools

- Wire cutters
- Scissors
- Low melt glue gun/glue sticks

Instructions

1 Mini delphiniums. Cut stems below bottom blossoms. Wire the stems together to form a 25" circle (or a circle to fit the size of the head).

2 Remaining flowers. Hot glue the open rose over a place where two stems meet. Hot glue pieces of snowball and a few hydrangea flowers around the rose and around the rest of the garland.

3 Green, pink and white ribbons. Using the green and white ribbons, make two 7" wide 2 loop Loopy bows with 24" and 12" tails. (See page 24.) Using the pink ribbon, make a 4" wide 2 loop Loopy bow with one 19" and one 9" tail. Wire the three bows together, and hot glue them to the garland under the open rose.

Materials

SWAG

- 36" Plumosa Garland (or wire 6 pkgs. of plumosus together)
- 1 Stem (pink) open rose
- 2 Stems (purple) hydrangeas
- 3 Stems (white) hydrangeas
- 2 Stems (white) wild roses
- 2 Yards (pink) 2" sheer ribbon
- ⅓ Yard (pink) dotted netting
- 4 Yards (peach) 2" wired ribbon
- Floral wire (light weight)

Tools

- Wire cutters
- Scissors
- Low melt glue gun/glue sticks

Instructions

1 Swag and all the flowers. Cut the flower stems to 2" long. Hot glue the rose in the middle, two wild roses next to it and the remaining wild roses at the ends of the swag. Cut the hydrangeas into 3-5 flower sections, and glue randomly throughout swag (front and back).

2 Netting. Cut two 6" X 36" strips of netting, and make two 12" wide, 2 loop Loopy bows with 6" tails (see page 25). Set aside.

3 Netting bows, peach and sheer ribbon. Make two 12" wide, 2 loop Loopy bows with 6" tails using the peach ribbon. Cut the sheer ribbon and the remaining peach ribbon in half, and wire a piece of each ribbon to each peach bow for streamers. Wire the peach bows to the netting bows, and wire the layered bows to the ends of the swag.

BRIDESMAID'S HEADPIECE & BOUQUET

Materials

HEADPIECE

- *2 Yards (off white) wired ribbon*
- *3" comb*
- *4 Pearl loops*

Tools

- *Scissors*
- *Low melt glue gun/glue sticks*

1 Ribbon. Make a 7" wide, 8 loop Loopy bow with 8" tails (see page 25). Set aside.

2 Comb and pearl loops. Wrap the stems of the pearl loops around the teeth of the comb. Position one on either end and two in the middle leaning forward and backwards.

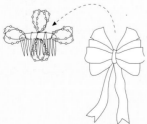

3 Bow. Hot glue the bow to the comb, and arrange the pearl loops in-between the bow loops.

Materials

BOUQUET

- *1 Stem (peach) open rose*
- *3 Stems plumosus fern*
- *7 Pearl sprays*
- *3 Stems dried (purple) baby's breath*
- *3½ Yards (pink) 2" wide sheer ribbon*
- *2 Yards (white) 2" wide sheer wire edge ribbon*
- *Floral wire (light weight)*
- *Floral tape*

Tools

- *Wire cutters*
- *Scissors*
- *Low melt glue gun/glue sticks*

1 Rose, baby's breath, pearl sprays and plumosus. Cut the rose to 8" tall. Surround the rose with pieces of baby's breath, pearl sprays and plumosus. Secure the top of the stems with floral wire. Cut the stems even at the bottom. The stem "handle" is 4" long.

2 Pink ribbon, floral wire and tape. Wrap the stems with floral wire and floral tape. Cut off a 12" piece of ribbon, and wrap the stems (see page 24). With the remaining pink ribbon, make a simple 11" wide, 2 loop Loopy bow with 24" and 27" tails. Glue to the top of the stems under the rose.

3 White ribbon. Make a 9" wide, 4 loop Florist bow, with 12" and 16" tails (see page 25). Hot glue to center of pink bow.

Men's Boutonniere

Materials

- *1 Stem (white) partly open rosebud*
- *1 Stem plumosus fern*
- *Floral tape (green)*
- *Floral wire*
- *1 Corsage pin*

Tools

- *Wire cutters*

Instructions

1 Rose. Cut rose stem to 1½" long.

2 Fern. Cut fern to 5" long.

3 All materials. Lay rose bud on top of fern and wire the two together. Cover the wire with floral tape (see page 24).

MOTHER'S CORSAGE

Materials

- 1 Stem (off white) medium open rose
- 2 Stems plumosus fern
- 1 Stem (purple) honeysuckle (or small amount of any small flowers)
- 1 Yard 1" wide, sheer, gold, wire edge ribbon
- Floral wire (light weight)
- Floral tape (white)

Tools

- Scissors
- Wire cutters
- Low melt glue gun/glue sticks

1 All flowers and fern. Lay the plumosus on a table. Lay the small flowers and the rose on top. Wire the stems under the rose. Cut the stems to 4" long.

2 Ribbon, florist wire and tape. Wire the length of the stems, and tape them tightly together. Cut off a 12" piece of ribbon, and wrap the stems (see page 24). Make a 6" wide, 4 loop Florist bow with 3" tails (see page 25). Hot glue the bow to the top of the stems under the flowers.

Ring Bearer's Pillow

Materials

- ¾ Yard (white) satin (45" wide)
- 10" X 10" pillow
- 2 Rings
- 5 Satin roses
- Small amount of tiny flowers
- 2 Yards 1/8" wide (ivory) ribbon
- 2 Bridal pearl and flower sprays (15" long)
- Floral wire (light weight)

Tools

- Scissors
- Iron
- Low melt glue gun/glue sticks

1 Fabric and pillow. Iron the fabric. Place the pillow in the center of the fabric. Fold the top and bottom sides over the pillow. Pull the ends up, and tie a knot in the center. Cut the ends to 12" long. Wire the ends of the "tails", tuck them under to form loops (like a bow), and hot glue to secure.

Instructions

2 Ribbon and rings. Cut the ribbon in half and glue the center of each piece under the "bow". Tie the rings to the ribbon

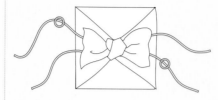

3 Pearl and flower sprays, roses and small flowers. Hot glue the ends of the sprays under the "bow". Cut the stems of the roses to 2" tall, and glue them around the "bow".

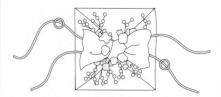

Headbands

Materials

- 1" Satin headband
- 1 Satin rose (3" wide) with pips in the center
- 1 Flower spray with pearls (6 flowers each)

Tools

- Low melt glue gun/glue sticks

Instructions

1. All the materials. Twist the stem of the rose around the center of the flower spray. Arrange the flowers and leaves around the rose.

2. Rose. Hot glue the rose 3" from the end of the headband. Lightly glue two of the leaves to the headband to secure the flowers.

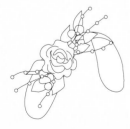

Note: This headband is a Lotus California, Inc. design and can be purchased at a craft store as a kit with instructions.

Materials

- 20" Tall Berdestone pedestal vase
- 1 Floral foam (green)
- 4 Stems (purple) wisteria
- 5 Stems (green/white) hydrangeas
- 6 Stems (pink) open roses
- 3 Stems (pink) poppies
- 2 Stems (pink) peonies
- 2 Stems (white) baby's breath
- 2 Stems (pink) mini daisies
- 3 Stems (purple) ranunculas
- 3 Stems (purple) day lilies

Tools

- Wire cutters

Note: Measure from top of flowers to cut stems.

Note: Substitute with similar flowers if those listed are not available.

Call: Aldik Artificial Flowers, Inc. for information about Berdestone products. (805)295-0170.

Instructions

1 Floral foam. Cut foam to fit snugly in vase. Fill vase with excess foam.

2 Wisteria. Cut flowers 25" tall from top bloom to end of stem.

ALL ILLUSTRATIONS ARE TOP VIEW SHOWING POSITION OF FLOWERS IN FOAM.

3 Hydrangeas. All are 9" tall.

4 Roses. Cut to 10", 10", 10", 11", 11" and 12".

5 Poppies. Cut to 10", 12" and 14" tall.

6 Peonies. All are 11" tall.

7 Baby's breath. Cut to 12" and 16" tall.

8 Mini daisies. Cut to 14" tall.

9 Ranunculas. Cut to 11" tall

10 Day lilies. Cut to 10" tall.